US COAST GUARD

BY SUE GAGLIARDI

Apex is distributed by North Star Editions:
sales@northstareditions.com | 888-417-0195

Produced for Apex by Red Line Editorial.

Photographs ©: Shutterstock Images, cover, 1, 4–5, 6, 7, 15, 19, 20–21, 22–23, 24–25, 26, 26–27, 29; iStockphoto, 8–9, 16–17, 18; 19th Era/Alamy Stock Photo, 10–11; John Moakley/Wikimedia Commons, 12–13

Library of Congress Control Number: 2022901412

ISBN
978-1-63738-312-4 (hardcover)
978-1-63738-348-3 (paperback)
978-1-63738-416-9 (ebook pdf)
978-1-63738-384-1 (hosted ebook)

Printed in the United States of America
Mankato, MN
082022

NOTE TO PARENTS AND EDUCATORS

Apex books are designed to build literacy skills in striving readers. Exciting, high-interest content attracts and holds readers' attention. The text is carefully leveled to allow students to achieve success quickly. Additional features, such as bolded glossary words for difficult terms, help build comprehension.

TABLE OF CONTENTS

CHAPTER 1

RESCUE AT SEA

A ship is sinking off the coast. Huge waves sweep people overboard. The water is freezing cold. The people are in danger.

The Coast Guard helps save people from emergencies on the water.

The Coast Guard uses helicopters for different missions.

HELICOPTER HELP

The Coast Guard can save people with helicopters. The helicopters fly above ships. Guardsmen lower themselves down on ropes. They lift the people to safety.

Coast Guard boats can move quickly through rough waters.

The captain sends out a **distress signal**. The Coast Guard responds. It sends a boat to help.

A rescue team swims out to the sinking ship. The rescuers pull people out of the water. They bring the people to the Coast Guard boat. They save the ship's entire crew.

FAST FACT

The Coast Guard's motto is "Always Ready."

The Coast Guard saves about 4,000 lives every year.

CHAPTER 2

COAST GUARD HISTORY

The Coast Guard was founded in 1790. It was first called the Revenue Cutter Service. Its job was to **patrol** the coast. It kept people from **smuggling** goods.

Early Coast Guard members caught people who broke the law.

Lighthouses stood near coasts. Their bright lights helped keep ships from hitting rocks.

A separate group did rescues. It was called the Life-Saving Service. In 1915, the two services combined. They became the Coast Guard. Later, the Coast Guard ran lighthouses, too. They guided ships during storms.

Coast Guard members have fought in wars, too. Their ships brought soldiers and supplies to battles.

WOMEN IN THE COAST GUARD

Women first worked for the Coast Guard in 1941. But they only did office jobs. Later, women joined the Coast Guard Reserves. In 1974, women were finally able to become guard members.

The US Coast Guard helped sink German submarines during World War II (1939–1945). ▶

CHAPTER 3

INSIDE THE COAST GUARD

Coast Guard members work at stations. Some stations are in the United States. Others are around the world.

One Coast Guard station is in Miami, Florida.

An officer leads each station. Air stations hold helicopters and other aircraft. Most stations use boats. Guard members go out on the water. They sail for a few days or weeks.

Each Coast Guard officer is in charge of a group of guardsmen.

Sammy the Sea Otter is a mascot for the Coast Guard. Sammy helps teach people about boat safety.

FAST FACT

Some Coast Guard stations have **mascots**. Mascots may go on rescues or patrols.

To join the Coast Guard, people do eight weeks of training. Guard members must be strong swimmers. They practice rescues. They learn first aid and firefighting, too.

Coast Guard members do rescues in all kinds of weather.

COAST GUARD CAREERS

Coast Guard members can train for many jobs. Some members fix aircraft or boats. Others give health care. Some are chefs.

CHAPTER 4

COAST GUARD MISSIONS

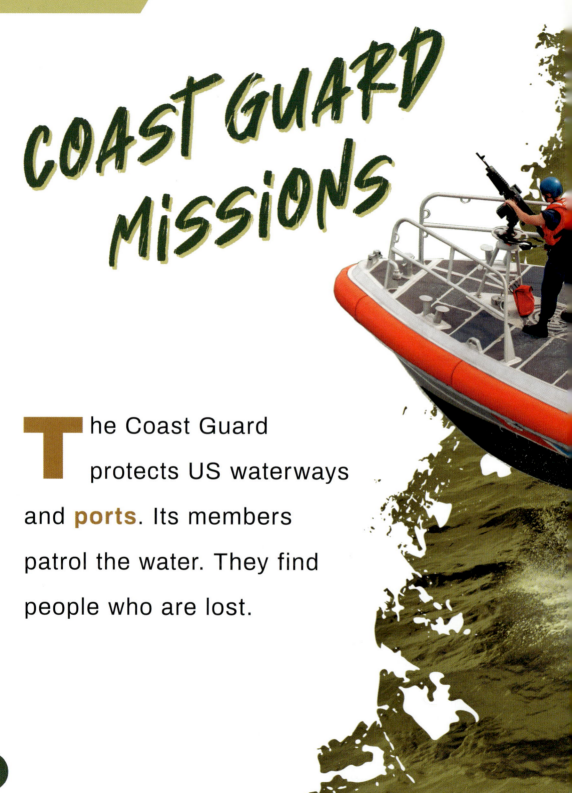

The Coast Guard protects US waterways and **ports**. Its members patrol the water. They find people who are lost.

U.S. COAST GUARD

Coast Guard ships sail on rivers, lakes, and oceans.

The US Coast Guard helps make sure waterways are safe for everyone to use.

U.S. COAST GUARD

107

The Coast Guard also makes sure people follow laws. It stops people from entering the United States **illegally**. It also defends the country from attacks.

FAST FACT

Catching some kinds of fish is illegal. The Coast Guard stops people from catching them.

The Coast Guard protects the environment, too. Its members may clean up oil spills. Or they may remove trash or **debris** after storms.

Coast Guard members clean up after Hurricane Sandy in 2012.

ICE PATROL

The Coast Guard runs an International Ice Patrol. Members keep track of icebergs in the Atlantic and Arctic Oceans. Then they help ships travel through the cold waters.

The Coast Guard breaks up ice to make paths for supply ships.

COMPREHENSION QUESTIONS

Write your answers on a separate piece of paper.

1. Write a sentence describing one job that Coast Guard members do.

2. Would you rather work on a helicopter or a boat? Why?

3. When were women able to join the Coast Guard as guard members?

　　A. 1939

　　B. 1941

　　C. 1974

4. Why do Coast Guard members need to be strong swimmers?

　　A. so they don't need to use boats

　　B. so they can save people in the water

　　C. so they can go to waterparks

5. What does **rescuers** mean in this book?

A rescue team swims out to the sinking ship. The rescuers pull people out of the water.

    A. people who are in danger

    B. people who save others

    C. people who hurt others

6. What does **responds** mean in this book?

The captain sends out a distress signal. The Coast Guard responds. It sends a boat to help.

    A. does nothing

    B. fights against something

    C. answers something

Answer key on page 32.

GLOSSARY

coast

The area where the land meets the sea.

debris

Pieces of something that broke or fell apart.

distress signal

Light, smoke, or sound used to call for help.

illegally

In a way that is against the law.

mascots

Animals, people, or things that bring good luck to groups.

patrol

To watch an area and keep it safe.

ports

Places along waterways where ships load and unload goods.

reserves

Groups of people who serve as backup or volunteers.

smuggling

Illegally taking goods into or out of a country.

TO LEARN MORE

BOOKS

London, Martha. *US Coast Guard Equipment and Vehicles.* Minneapolis: Abdo Publishing, 2021.

Morey, Allan. *U.S. Coast Guard.* Minneapolis: Jump!, 2021.

Vonder Brink, Tracy. *The United States Coast Guard.* North Mankato, MN: Capstone Publishing, 2021.

ONLINE RESOURCES

Visit **www.apexeditions.com** to find links and resources related to this title.

ABOUT THE AUTHOR

Sue Gagliardi writes fiction, nonfiction, and poetry for children. She is a teacher and lives in Pennsylvania with her husband and son.

INDEX

ANSWER KEY:
1. Answers will vary; 2. Answers will vary; 3. C; 4. B; 5. B; 6. C